VIRTUE STORIES

# Do it Yourself

Lalita Iyer

Om KIDZ
An imprint of Om Books International

'Please fasten your seatbelts.' The pilot said, 'The plane will be landing shortly.'

Nadine was very excited. It was the first time she was visiting New York. She had been looking forward to meeting her aunt and cousins all summer!

On reaching their aunt's house, her two cousins - Dan and Sam, raced to the car even before they had barely stepped out of it.

Everyone went inside, chattering away, looking happy.

Nadine went to her room to freshen up and then went down for dinner. ‘Nadine, be a doll and take these plates to the dining room, will you? I don’t know where Sam and Dan have disappeared.’ Her aunt said, looking absolutely exhausted as she stirred something in a big vessel.

This was very puzzling. You see, Nadine was from Mumbai and like most of the rich people from Mumbai she had house help commonly known as 'servants'.

This meant that Nadine never had to do any work! Everything was taken care of, by the help. She had never ever laid a table in her life!

However, in America, most people couldn't afford house help. They did everything all by themselves!

Nadine took the plates, anyway; And then she took the spoons and forks; and then the table mats; and then the food. *This laying the table thing was kind of fun.*

When they all sat down for dinner, the table looked different. Nadine couldn't help admiring herself at what a good job she had done. It felt nice to have done something without the help.

This was fun. I wonder why they call it chores, she wondered. She now looked forward to what else she could do to help Aunt Naomi. And there was plenty!

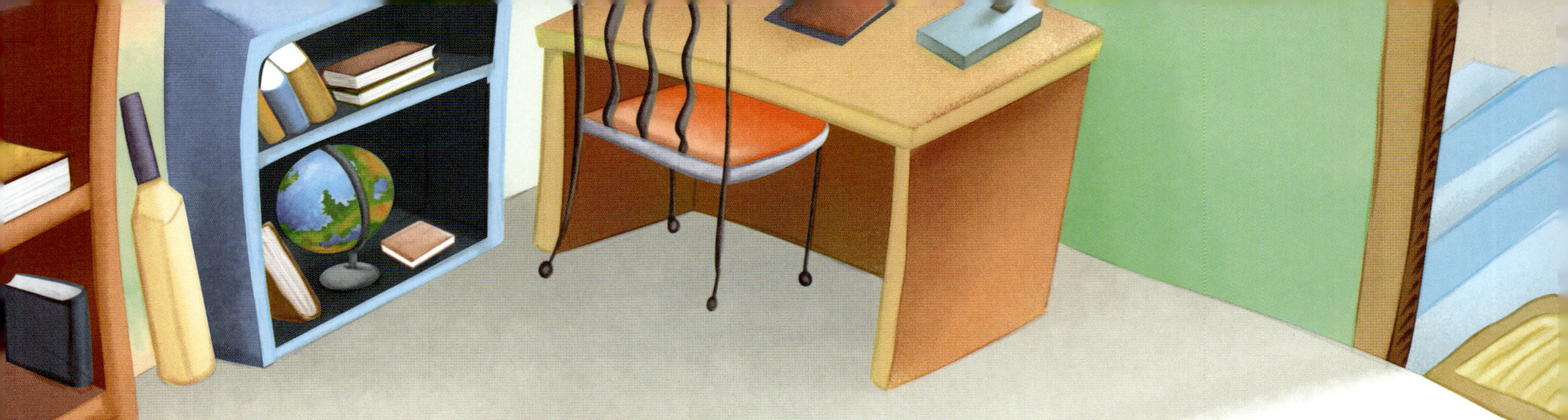

Every day, she would hang out her wet towels to dry, she'd fold her own clothes and make her own bed. After every task she did, she felt a little thrill. She resolved that when she went back home after her holidays in America, she would do the same. The help needed a break too!

Nadine had finally begun doing things by herself and what a joy that was!